Dad Jokes

Dad Jokes

More than **400** Unbearable, Groan-inducing One-Liners Sure to Make You the Deadliest Dad with a Pun

— Joe Kerz —

Racehorse Publishing

Racehorse Publishing books may be purchased in bulk at special discounts for sales promotion, corporate gifts, fund-raising, or educational purposes. Special editions can also be created to specifications. For details, contact the Special Sales Department, Skyhorse Publishing, 307 West 36th Street, 11th Floor, New York, NY 10018 or info@skyhorsepublishing.com.

Racehorse Publishing™ is a pending trademark of Skyhorse Publishing, Inc.®, a Delaware corporation.

Visit our website at www.skyhorsepublishing.com.

10 9 8 7 6 5 4 3 2

Library of Congress Cataloging-in-Publication Data is available on file.

Cover illustration by iStockphoto/Vect0r0vich
Interior art by iStockphoto

ISBN: 978-1-63158-372-8
E-Book ISBN: 978-1-63158-373-5

Printed in the United States of America

INTRODUCTION

As if being a father wasn't hard enough, now you have to be funny as well? It's a high-pressure situation. Thankfully, some genius fathers must have gotten together and realized that they had to right the ship, and this book provides you smooth sailing even if you are a novice at the pun game.

There's plenty here to dig into. Grab your shovel. The great thing about the Dad Joke is that it gives you the opportunity to revolt in your own way. How many things have you been asked to fix today that you simply don't know how to fix? How many times did you have to make room for the kids sleeping in your bed only to find your-self eventually displaced to the couch? Now, it's time for revenge. Make the kids cringe; be spectacularly uncool.

Each and every one of these jokes enclosed in this tome are sure to illicit a response. None of these responses may be laughter, but there will surely be a reaction! The more eye-rolling and forehead-slapping, the better. If all goes well you'll hear an annoyed statement of "*DAD!*" and you'll know you've done your job. Be sure to share the content of this book with other fathers. The time has come—get ready to unleash your corniest pun and worst groaner. Dad Jokes are no laughing matter.

JOKES

1

WHAT DID THE POLICEMAN SAY TO HIS BELLY BUTTON?

You're under a vest!

2

Why did the cookie go to the hospital?

Because he felt crummy!

3

Why did Billy throw the clock out of the window?

Because he wanted to see time fly!

4

WHAT DO LAWYERS WEAR TO COURT?

Lawsuits!

5

What do you call a fake noodle?

An impasta!

6

Why did the robber take a bath?

Because he wanted to make a clean getaway!

7

What did one toilet say to the other toilet?

You look flushed!

WHAT DO YOU CALL A BELT WITH A WATCH ON IT?

A waist of time!

How do you find a Princess?

You follow the foot Prince.

10

What lights up a soccer stadium?

A soccer match!

11

Where do snowmen keep their money?

In snow banks!

12

WHY SHOULDN'T YOU WRITE WITH A BROKEN PENCIL?

Because it's pointless!

13

Why did the man put his money in the freezer?

He wanted cold hard cash!

What lies at the bottom of the ocean and twitches?

A nervous wreck!

How do you make a tissue dance?

Put a little boogey in it!

16

What do you call a sleeping bull?

A bulldozer!

17

Why was the student's report card wet?

It was below C level!

18

Why wouldn't the shrimp share his treasure?

Because he was a little shellfish!

19

What do you call bears with no ears?

B.

20

What did the judge say when the skunk walked in the court room?

Odor in the court.

21

HOW MANY TICKLES DOES IT TAKE TO MAKE AN OCTOPUS LAUGH?

Ten-tickles.

22

What do you call the heavy breathing someone makes while trying to hold a yoga pose?

Yoga pants.

23

WHAT IS THE BEST DAY TO GO TO THE BEACH?

Sunday, of course!

24

How do hens cheer for their team?

They egg them on!

25

Why did the man with one hand cross the road?

To get to the second-hand shop.

26

WHEN DOES FRIDAY COME BEFORE THURSDAY?

In the dictionary!

27

How does NASA organize a party?

They planet.

28

What bow can't be tied?

A rainbow!

29

Why did the birdie go to the hospital?

To get a tweetment.

30

What has one head, one foot, and four legs?

A Bed.

31

Where did the computer go to dance?

To a disc-o.

32

WHY DID THE BANANA GO TO THE DOCTOR?

Because it was not peeling well.

33

Why is England the wettest country?

Because the queen has reigned there for years!

Why did the computer go to the doctor?

Because it had a virus!

Why did Roger go out with a prune?

Because he couldn't find a date!

36

What happened to the dog that swallowed a firefly?

It barked with de-light!

37

WHO EARNS A LIVING DRIVING THEIR CUSTOMERS AWAY?

A taxi driver.

HOW DO YOU SHOOT A KILLER BEE?

With a bee-bee gun.

Did you hear about the restaurant on the moon?

Great food, no atmosphere!

Want to hear a joke about paper?

Nevermind, it's tearable.

Why did the coffee file a police report?

It got mugged.

42

What do you call an elephant that doesn't matter?

An irrelephant.

43

WHY DON'T SKELETONS EVER GO TRICK OR TREATING?

Because they have no body to go with.

44

What did one snowman say to the other one?

Do you smell carrots?

45

Did you hear about the man who stole a calendar?

He got 12 months.

Where can you get chicken broth in bulk?

The Stock Market.

What do you call a man with no nose and no body?

Nobody nose.

48

How much does a hipster weigh?

An Instagram.

49

What did the daddy tomato say to the baby tomato?

Catch up!

50

WHAT'S FORREST GUMP'S PASSWORD?

1forrest1.

51

Why did the scarecrow win an award?

Because he was outstanding in his field.

Why shouldn't you buy anything with Velcro on it?

It's a total rip-off!

What did Winnie The Pooh say to his agent?

Show me the honey!

What goes through towns, up and over hills, but doesn't move?

The road!

What kind of dogs like car racing?

Lap dogs.

56

Why was there thunder and lightning in the lab?

The scientists were brainstorming!

57

WHY COULDN'T THE PIRATE PLAY CARDS?

Because he was sitting on the deck!

58

WHAT DO YOU CALL A BABY MONKEY?

A chimp off the old block.

59

Where do bees go to the bathroom?

At the BP station!

60

What did the blanket say to the bed?

Don't worry, I've got you covered!

61

Why did the traffic light turn red?

You would too if you had to change in the middle of the street!

What did one elevator say to the other elevator?

I think I'm coming down with something!

What do you get when you cross fish and an elephant?

Swimming trunks.

64

WHAT DO CALL CHEESE THAT ISN'T YOURS?

Nacho Cheese!

65

What kind of bird sticks to sweaters?

A Vel-Crow.

66

What washes up on very small beaches?

Microwaves.

67

WHAT KIND OF CRACKERS DO FIREMEN LIKE IN THEIR SOUP?

Firecrackers!

What did the digital clock say to the grandfather clock?

Look grandpa, no hands!

What is an astronaut's favorite place on a computer?

The space bar!

70

Which month do soldiers hate most?

The month of March!

71

What did the judge say to the dentist?

Do you swear to pull the tooth, the whole tooth, and nothing but the tooth?

72

What starts with a P, ends with an E, and has a million letters in it?

Post Office!

73

WHICH U.S. STATE HAS THE SMALLEST SOFT DRINKS?

Mini-soda.

74

Why did the stadium get hot after the game?

All of the fans left.

75

WHAT DID THE DUCK SAY TO THE BARTENDER?

Put it on my bill.

76

How does a squid go into battle?

Well-armed.

77

What kind of tea is hard to swallow?

Reality.

Why was the guy looking for fast food on his friend?

Because his friend said dinner is on me.

What did the time traveler do when he was still hungry after his last bite?

He went back four seconds.

80

What do you call an unpredictable, out-of-control photographer?

A loose Canon.

81

DID YOU HEAR ABOUT THE SENSITIVE BURGLAR?

He takes things personally.

82

Did the disappointed smoker get everything he wanted for Christmas?

Clothes, but no cigar.

83

What do you call the sound a dog makes when it's choking on a piece of its owner's jewelry?

A diamond in the ruff.

84

WHY DID THE YOGURT GO TO THE ART EXHIBIT?

Because it was cultured.

85

Where do cows hang their paintings?

In the mooo-seum.

86

WHY DID THE TOMATO TURN RED?

Because it saw the salad dressing!

87

Why did the can crusher quit his job?

Because it was soda pressing.

What do bees do if they want to use public transport?

Wait at a buzz stop!

What did the fashion police officer say to his sweater?

"Do you know why I pulled you over?"

90

WHAT'S THE MOST MUSICAL PART OF A CHICKEN?

The drumstick.

91

Why was the baby strawberry crying?

Because his mom and dad were in a jam!

92

What did the fisherman say to the magician?

Pick a cod, any cod!

93

**What did the red light say
to the green light?**

Don't look, I'm changing!

94

Why couldn't the sesame seed leave the casino?

Because he was on a roll.

95

What would Bears be without Bees?

Ears.

96

Why did the poor man sell yeast?

To raise some dough.

97

HOW DO SNAILS FIGHT?

They slug it out.

98

Why do bananas wear suntan lotion?

Because they peel.

99

What's the difference between ignorance and apathy?

I don't know and I don't care.

100

WHY ARE PENGUINS SOCIALLY AWKWARD?

Because they can't break the ice.

101

Where do hamburgers go to dance?

They go to the meat-ball.

102

WHAT KIND OF SHOES DO ALL SPIES WEAR?

Sneakers.

103

Why did the boy tiptoe past the medicine cabinet?

He didn't want to wake the sleeping pills!

104

What do you get when you put your radio in the fridge?

Cool music.

105

Why did the belt go to jail?

Because it held up a pair of pants!

106

What do you call a bear with no socks on?

Bare-foot.

107

WHAT CAN YOU SERVE BUT NEVER EAT?

A volleyball.

108

Why did the boy sprinkle sugar on his pillow before he went to sleep?

So he could have sweet dreams.

109

What did the penny say to the other penny?

We make perfect cents.

110

Why did the hipster burn his tongue with his pizza?

He ate it before it was cool!

111

How do crazy people go through the forest?

They take the psycho path.

112

What do you call an apology written in dots and dashes?

Remorse code.

113

WHAT DO YOU CALL A FAT PSYCHIC?

A four-chin teller.

114

WHY AREN'T KOALAS ACTUAL BEARS?

The don't meet the koalafications.

115

What's brown and sticky?

A stick.

116

What's a foot long and slippery?

A slipper.

117

What's red and moves up and down?

A tomato in an elevator.

118

What do Alexander the Great and Winnie the Pooh have in common?

Same middle name.

119

Who walks into a restaurant, eats shoots and leaves?

A Panda.

120

WHAT DID ONE EYE SAY TO THE OTHER EYE?

Don't look now, but something between us smells.

121

What streets do ghosts haunt?

Dead ends!

122

WHAT DO YOU CALL IT WHEN BATMAN SKIPS CHURCH?

Christian Bale.

123

What did the grape do when it got stepped on?

It let out a little wine!

What did the time traveler do when he was still hungry after dinner?

He went back four seconds.

How many lips does a flower have?

Tu-lips.

126

What do you call a shoe made out of a banana?

A slipper.

127

WHY COULDN'T THE TOILET PAPER CROSS THE ROAD?

Because it got stuck in a crack.

How much does a pirate pay for corn?

A buccaneer.

What did the mayonnaise say when the refrigerator door was opened?

Close the door, I'm dressing.

How do you stop a bull from charging?

Cancel its credit card.

What's a skeleton's favorite musical instrument?

The trom-bone.

132

What disease do you get when you put up the Christmas decorations?

Tinselitus.

133

HOW DO BILLBOARDS TALK?

Sign language.

134

What do you get when you cross a snowman with a vampire?

Frostbite.

135

Why was the sand wet?

Because the sea weed.

HOW DID THE BARBER
WIN THE RACE?

He knew a short cut.

**What's orange and sounds
like a parrot?**

A carrot.

138

When is a door not a door?

When it's ajar.

139

WHY IS CORN SUCH A GOOD LISTENER?

Because it's all ears.

140

What do you call a pile of cats?

A meow-ntain.

141

Why did the golfer wear two pairs of pants?

In case he got a hole in one.

142

Why did the chicken cross the playground?

To get to the other slide.

143

What did the first plate say to the second plate?

Dinner's on me.

144

What did the football coach say to the broken vending machine?

Give me my quarterback.

145

WHY CAN'T YOU TRUST THE KING OF THE JUNGLE?

Because he's always lion.

146

WHEN IS A CAR NOT A CAR?

When it turns into a street.

147

How does a rancher keep track of his cattle?

With a cow-culator.

148

Have you heard about the pregnant bed bug?

She's going to have her baby in the spring.

149

What do you call a sleeping bull?

A bull-dozer.

150

Why is there a wall around the cemetery?

Because people are dying to get in.

151

Why could the bee not hear what people were saying?

He had wax in his ears.

152

WHAT'S E.T. SHORT FOR?

He's got little legs.

153

How do you make a Swiss roll?

Push him down a mountain.

154

What did the swordfish say to the marlin?

You're looking sharp.

155

WHAT DO OLYMPIC SPRINTERS EAT BEFORE A RACE?

Nothing. They fast.

156

What's a didgeridoo?

Whatever it wants to.

157

Did you hear about the sensitive burglar?

He takes things personally.

158

Why do cows wear bells?

Because their horns don't work.

159

How do you stop moles from digging in your garden?

Hide the spade.

160

DID YOU HEAR ABOUT THE ITALIAN CHEF WHO DIED.

He pasta way.

161

What does a nut say when it sneezes?

Cashew.

162

Why did Santa study music at college?

To improve his rapping skills.

163

How do you make a Venetian blind?

Poke him in the eyes.

164

WHAT DO YOU CALL CRYSTAL CLEAR URINE?

1080pee.

165

What do you call a group of disorganized cats?

A cat-astrophe.

166

WHY SHOULDN'T YOU PLAY CARDS ON THE SAVANNAH?

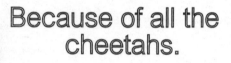

Because of all the cheetahs.

167

Did you hear about the population of Ireland's capital?

It's Dublin.

168

How do you impress a female baker?

Bring her flours.

169

Why did the bicycle fall over?

Because it was two tired.

170

Why did the mobile phone need glasses?

It lost all its contacts.

171

What did the hat say to the scarf?

You go ahead, I'll hang around.

172

WHAT DID THE BABY CORN SAY TO THE MAMA CORN?

Where's pop corn?

173

What did the chip say when he saw the cheese stealing?

Hey, that's Nachos.

174

WHAT DO YOU CALL A BOAT WITH A HOLE IN THE BOTTOM?

A sink.

175

Why do seagulls fly over the sea?

Because if they flew over the bay they'd be called bagels.

176

What kind of music do mummies listen to?

Wrap music.

177

Why did the cookie go to the doctors?

Because he felt crummy.

178

Why did the stadium get hot after the game?

All the fans left.

179

Why do bananas wear sunscreen?

To stop them from peeling.

180

What's the difference between America and a memory stick?

One's USA and the other's USB.

181

WHAT DO YOU CALL AN ESCAPED OWL?

Hoodini.

182

WHAT DID THE BIG CHIMNEY SAY TO THE LITTLE CHIMNEY?

You're too young to smoke.

183

What's a bear with no teeth called?

A gummy bear.

184

Why couldn't the bad sailor learn his alphabet?

Because he always got lost at C.

185

What did the first street say to the second street?

I'll meet you at the intersection.

Why are teddy bears never hungry?

Because they're always stuffed.

What did one toilet say to the other toilet?

You look flushed.

188

WHAT'S THE BEST TIME TO GO TO THE DENTIST?

Tooth hurty.

189

What do you call a factory that makes good products?

A satis-factory.

189

WHICH SIDE OF A DUCK HAS THE MOST FEATHERS?

The outside.

190

Where do Volkswagens go when they get old?

The old Volks home.

200

What do a dog and a phone have in common?

They both have collar ID.

201

What did the red light say to the green light?

Don't look, I'm changing.

202

What do you call a T-Rex that's been beaten up?

Dino-sore.

203

What did the axe murderer say to the judge?

It was an axe-ident.

204

HOW MUCH DOES A MUSTANG COST?

More than you can af-Ford.

205

What do you call someone who plays tricks on Halloween?

Prankenstein.

206

WHY CAN'T YOUR NOSE BE TWELVE INCHES LONG?

Because then it'd be a foot.

207

Why did the pig get hired by the restaurant?

He was really good at bacon.

208

What do you call anxious dinosaurs?

Nervous Rex.

209

What do you call a snobbish criminal going down the stairs?

A condescending con descending.

210

Did you hear about the kidnapping at school?

He woke up.

211

I'M LIKE THE FABRIC VERSION OF KING MIDAS.

Everything I touch becomes felt.

212

My wife first agreed to a date after I gave her a bottle of tonic water.

I Schwepped her of her feet.

213

I always used to get small shocks when touching metal objects, but it recently stopped.

Needless to say, I'm ex-static.

214

Why do Norwegians build their own tables?

No Ikea!

215

WHY DID THE COFFEE GO TO THE POLICE?

It got mugged.

216

How many ears does Captain Kirk have?

Three: the left ear, the right ear, and the final frontier.

217

I knew I shouldn't have had the sea food.

I'm feeling a little eel.

218

**What's made of brass and sounds
like Tom Jones?**

Trombones.

219

What do prisoners use to call each other?

Cell phones.

220

What do you call an old person with really good hearing?

Deaf-defying.

221

MY WIFE KEEPS TELLING ME TO STOP PRETENDING TO BE BUTTER.

But I'm on a roll now.

How does Darth Vader like his toast?

On the dark side.

I'm the Norse god of mischief, but I don't like to talk about it.

I guess you could say I'm low-key.

224

My wife says she's leaving me because she thinks I'm too obsessed with astronomy.

What planet is she on!

225

WHAT KIND OF TEA DO YOU DRINK WITH THE QUEEN?

Royal tea.

THE CIRCLE IS JUST THE MOST RIDICULOUS SHAPE IN THE WORLD.

There's absolutely no point to it.

There's been an explosion at a cheese factory in Paris.

There's nothing left but de Brie.

228

Last night, I had a dream that I was a muffler.

I woke up exhausted.

229

What are bald sea captains most worried about?

Cap sizes.

230

When is a cow hairy on the inside and the outside at the same time?

When it's stood in the doorway of the barn.

231

Where do you learn to make ice cream?

At sundae school.

232

Who was the roundest knight at King Arthur's round table?

Sir Cumference.

233

IF PRISONERS COULD TAKE THEIR OWN MUG SHOTS, WOULD THEY BE CALLED CELLFIES?

234

Why do chicken coops only have two doors?

Because if they had four doors, they'd be chicken sedans.

235

DOGS CAN'T OPERATE MRI MACHINES, BUT CATSCAN.

236

Did you hear about the restaurant on the moon?

Great food, no atmosphere.

237

My son must have been relieved to have finally been born.

He looked like he was running out of womb in there.

238

What do you call a snowman with a six pack?

An abdominal snowman.

239

My mom bought me a really cheap dictionary for my birthday.

I couldn't find the words to thank her.

240

HOW MANY APPLES GROW ON A TREE?

All of them.

241

What do you call an explosive horse?

Neigh-palm.

I tried to have a conversation with my wife when she was applying a mud pack.

You should have seen the filthy look she gave me.

WHAT DO YOU CALL A HORSE THAT MOVES AROUND A LOT?

Unstable.

244

I just texted my girlfriend Ruth and told her that it's over between us.

I'm Ruthless.

245

What type of magazines do cows read?

Cattlelogs.

246

WHAT DO YOU CALL A COW THAT JUST HAD A BABY?

DeCALFeinated or A New Moother

247

RIP boiled water. You will be mist.

248

I don't trust stairs.

They're always up to something.

249

IF YOU WANT A JOB IN THE MOISTURIZER INDUSTRY, THE BEST ADVICE I CAN GIVE IS TO APPLY DAILY.

I hate perforated lines.

They're tearable.

WHEN MY WIFE TOLD ME TO STOP IMPERSONATING A FLAMINGO, I HAD TO PUT MY FOOT DOWN.

252

What do you call a can of soup that eats other cans of soup?

A CANnibal.

253

Why can't you hear a pterodactyl using the bathroom?

Because the P is silent.

254

THE ROTATION OF EARTH REALLY MAKES MY DAY.

255

Want to hear a joke about construction?

Nah, I'm still working on it.

256

You heard the rumor going around about butter?

Nevermind, I shouldn't spread it.

257

WHAT CONCERT COSTS ONLY 45 CENTS?

50 Cent ft. Nickelback.

What do they call Miley Cyrus in Europe?

Kilometry Cyrus.

I HAVE KLEPTOMANIA.

Sometimes when it gets really bad, I take something for it.

260

YOU SHOULDN'T KISS ANYONE ON JANUARY 1ST BECAUSE IT'S ONLY THE FIRST DATE.

261

If a child refuses to take a nap, is he resisting a rest?

262

What's the difference between a hippo and a zippo?

One is really heavy and the other is a little lighter.

263

WANT TO HEAR MY PIZZA JOKE?

Never mind, it's too cheesy.

264

What does a house wear?

A dress.

265

A furniture store keeps calling me.

But all I wanted was one night stand.

Why does Peter pan always fly?

Because he Neverlands!

My wife is on a tropical food diet; the house is full of the stuff.

It's enough to make a mango crazy.

268

MY WIFE TOLD ME I WAS AVERAGE, I THINK SHE'S MEAN.

269

Had seafood last night, now I'm eel.

270

I gave all my dead batteries away today . . .

Free of charge.

271

JUST QUIT MY JOB AT STARBUCKS BECAUSE DAY AFTER DAY IT WAS THE SAME OLD GRIND.

Went to the corner shop today . . .

Bought four corners.

How do you drown a hipster?

In the mainstream.

I'm thinking about getting a new haircut . . .

I'm going to mullet over.

Why couldn't the bicycle stand up by itself?

It was two tired.

276

WHAT DO YOU CALL SANTA'S HELPERS?

Subordinate clauses.

277

What time is it?

I don't know. It keeps changing.

278

A man knocked on my door and asked for a small donation for a local swimming pool.

So, I gave him a glass of water.

279

I went to a really emotional wedding the other day . . .

Even the cake was in tiers.

280

I was getting into my car the other day and a man asked: "Can you give me a lift?"

I said: "Sure, you look great, chase your dreams, go for it!"

281

MY WIFE AND I WERE HAPPY FOR TWENTY YEARS.

But then we met.

How do prisoners call each other?

On their cell phones!

Did you hear about the man who lost his entire left side in an accident?

He's all right now.

284

Claustrophobic people are more productive thinking outside the box.

285

PEOPLE WHO LACK THE PATIENCE FOR CALLIGRAPHY WILL NEVER HAVE PROPERLY FORMED CHARACTERS.

286

WAKING UP THIS MORNING WAS AN EYE-OPENING EXPERIENCE.

287

I tripped over my wife's bra.

It seemed to be a booby trap!

288

**She had a photographic memory,
but never developed it.**

289

MY MATH TEACHER CALLED ME AVERAGE. HOW MEAN!

290

SLEEPING COMES SO NATURALLY TO ME, I CAN DO IT WITH MY EYES CLOSED.

291

I had to quit my job at the shoe recycling factory.

It was just sole destroying.

292

Butchers link sausage to make ends meat.

293

WHY DIDN'T THE LIFEGUARD SAVE THE HIPPIE?

Because he was too far out, man.

294

A TRAIN STOPS AT A TRAIN STATION. A BUS STOPS AT A BUS STATION.

Now, why is my desk called a "work station?"

295

I used to be a banker, but over time I lost interest.

296

The girl quit her job at the donut factory because she was fed up with the hole business.

297

I went to a buffet dinner with my neighbor, who is a taxidermist.

After such a big meal, I was stuffed.

298

A lawyer-turned-cook is a sue chef.

299

THE FOOD THEY SERVE TO GUARDS CAN LAST FOR SENTRIES.

300

HOW DO CONSTRUCTION WORKERS PARTY? THEY RAISE THE ROOF.

301

Tree trimmers do such a fantastic job, they should take a bough.

302

The librarian didn't know what to do with the book about Tesla's love of electricity, so he filed it under "Current Affairs."

303

After manually rotating the heavy machinery, the worker grew pretty cranky.

304

The inept psychic attempted clairvoyance, but just couldn't get intuit.

305

THE CARPENTER CAME 'ROUND THE OTHER DAY.

He made the best entrance I have ever seen . . .

306

TELLING A DEMOLITIONIST HOW TO DO HIS JOB IS DESTRUCTIVE CRITICISM.

307

Old artists never retire, they withdraw instead!

308

The key to job searching is looking deep within yourself.

It's all about the inner view.

309

THE OBSTETRICIANS SEEM TO CELEBRATE LABOR DAY EVERY SINGLE DAY!

310

The pilot was a loner but even for him flying a drone was simply too remote.

311

WHAT TYPE OF SHIRT DOES AN ASTRONAUT WEAR?

Apollo shirt.

312

I slept like a log during the night shift and I was axed when I awoke!

313

The incompetent telegrapher was a weapon of Morse destruction.

314

A FRIEND OF MINE TRIED TO ANNOY ME WITH BIRD PUNS, BUT **I** SOON REALIZED THAT TOUCAN PLAY AT THAT GAME.

315

The deer grabbed the gun and gave the hunter a taste of his own venison.

316

Why did the bee get married?

Because he found his honey.

317

What did the buffalo say to his son when he left for college?

Bison.

318

WHY DO SEALS SWIM IN SALT WATER?

Because pepper water
makes them sneeze.

319

Pig puns are really boaring.

320

A dog gave birth to puppies at the roadside
and was fined for littering.

321

The best way to communicate with a fish is to
drop them a line.

322

CUDDLING A CAT USUALLY LEAVES YOU FELINE GOOD.

323

What do you call a magic dog?

A Labracadabrador.

324

What do you call bees that are fat?

Obeese.

325

What do you call a cow eating grass?

A lawn-mooer.

326

What city has the largest rodent population?

Hamsterdam.

327

I'VE GOT A CHICKEN-PROOF GARDEN. IT'S COMPLETELY IMPECCABLE!

328

What do you call a cow with two legs?

Lean beef.

329

Which day do chickens hate the most?

Fry-day.

330

WHAT DO YOU CALL AN ALLIGATOR IN A VEST?

Investigator.

331

Have you ever heard of an honest cheetah?

Why couldn't the chicken locate her eggs?

Because she had mislaid them.

What do you call a fish with no eyes?

A fsh.

334

Why are most horses so slim?

Because they are on a stable diet!

335

WHY DO COWS WEAR BELLS?

Because their horns don't work!

336

What kind of pumpkin protects castles?

A royal gourd!

337

Even covered in salad dressing my lettuce looked bare, so I put some cloves on it.

WHERE DO WITCHES BAKE THEIR CAKES?

In a coven.

Two loaves of bread wanted to get married, which is why they eloafed.

340

I get distracted by all the meats in the deli section, must be my short attention spam.

341

WHAT ARE TWINS' FAVORITE FRUIT?

Pears!

342

Did you hear the joke about the peanut butter?

I'm not telling you. You might spread it!

343

Who's the king of vegetables?

Elvis Parsley.

344

WHY DID THE STUDENTS EAT THEIR HOMEWORK?

Their teacher said it was a piece of cake.

345

What do you call an almond in space?

An astronut.

346

Why didn't the banana go to work?

It wasn't peeling well.

347

Why doesn't bread like warm weather?

Because it makes things toasty!

348

I always believed my body was a prison.

I was right, in biology, I learned it was made of cells.

349

THE SKELETON COMIC WAS TRYING TIBIA LITTLE HUMERUS.

Masks have no face value!

DOES MY BRAND-NEW SMILE DENTURE EGO?

352

MY FRIEND STARTED TELLING ME SKELETON PUNS.

They were all extremely rib-tickling.

353

How do you capture a skeleton?

Use a rib-cage.

354

I'm friends with my fist, even though he's quite a knuckle head.

355

THE CARDIOVASCULAR SYSTEM IS A WORK OF ARTERY, BUT IT IS ALSO PRETTY VEIN.

356

What did the bra say to the hat?

You go on a head while I give these two a lift.

357

Never date a tennis player.

Love means nothing to them.

358

I wondered why the baseball was getting bigger.

Then it hit me.

359

Why don't some couples go to the gym?

Because some relationships don't work out.

360

Do beginner vampires go to batting practice?

361

SINCE I QUIT SOCCER, I'VE LOST MY LIFE GOALS.

362

I lift weights only on Saturday and Sunday because Monday to Friday are weak days.

363

I'M NOT A HUGE FAN OF ARCHERY.

It has way too many drawbacks!

364

My snowboarding skills are really going downhill fast!

365

My tennis opponent was not happy with my service.

He kept returning it.

366

I quit gymnastics because I was fed up of hanging around the bars.

367

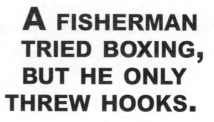

A FISHERMAN TRIED BOXING, BUT HE ONLY THREW HOOKS.

368

What should you say to impatient jockeys?

Hold your horses.

369

The race car driver had a pretty checkered past. . . .

370

Old skiers go downhill fast. . . .

371

THE WEIGH-IN AT THE SUMO WRESTLING CHAMPIONSHIP WAS A LARGE SCALE EFFORT.

372

Why was the referee fired?

Because he was a whistle blower!

373

After a long time waiting for the bowling alley to open, we eventually got the ball rolling.

374

I COULDN'T QUITE REMEMBER HOW TO THROW A BOOMERANG, BUT EVENTUALLY, IT CAME BACK TO ME.

375

Refusing to go to the gym counts as resistance training, right?

I'm taking part in a stair-climbing competition.

Guess I better step up my game.

Why do soccer players do so well in math?

They know how to use their heads!

378

Why was Cinderella banned from playing sports?

Because she always ran away from the ball.

379

I can't understand why people are so bothered about me not knowing what the word "apocalypse" means.

It's not like it's the end of the world!

380

I WAS THINKING ABOUT GETTING A BRAIN TRANSPLANT, BUT THEN I CHANGED MY MIND.

381

To the guy who invented zero:
Thanks for nothing!

382

WHERE DO BABY SPOONS COME FROM?

The spork delivers them.

383

The man's zipper broke, but he fixed it on the fly.

384

A hair-raising experience sounds promising to a bald man.

385

It was cold in the bedroom, so I laid down in the fireplace and slept like a log.

386

Don't spell "part" backwards.

It's a trap!

387

Why don't cannibals eat clowns?

They taste rather funny.

388

I recently got crushed by a pile of books, but I suppose I've only got my shelf to blame.

389

I've decided to sell my vacuum.

Well, it was just gathering dust!

390

I saw a documentary on how ships are kept together.

Riveting!

391

I've been reading a book about anti-gravity.

It's impossible to put down.

392

Have you heard about the magic tractor?

It turned into a field!

393

I couldn't work out how to fasten my seatbelt for ages.

But then one day, it just clicked.

394

Yesterday, I accidentally swallowed some food coloring.

The doctor says I'm OK, but I feel like I've dyed a little inside.

395

I'd tell you a chemistry joke, but I know I wouldn't get a reaction.

396

HAVE YOU EVER TRIED TO EAT A CLOCK?

It's very time-consuming.

397

I didn't use to like duct-tape at first, but I soon became attached to it.

The newspaper's rationale for running the story was paper thin.

I really wanted a camouflage cap, but I couldn't find one.

400

I planned to find my watch today, but I didn't have the time.

401

WHERE DID NOAH KEEP HIS BEES?

In the ark hives.